THE MIDDLE AGES

poems by

Raymond Berthelot

Finishing Line Press
Georgetown, Kentucky

THE MIDDLE AGES

Copyright © 2022 by Raymond Berthelot
ISBN 978-1-64662-848-3 First Edition
All rights reserved under International and Pan-American Copyright Conventions. No part of this book may be reproduced in any manner whatsoever without written permission from the publisher, except in the case of brief quotations embodied in critical articles and reviews.

ACKNOWLEDGMENTS

Grateful acknowledgement is due to the editors of the following journals, in which these poems first appeared:

Journal of Caribbean Literatures: "Ode to Fishermen"
The Carolina Quarterly: "Three Thrushes," "Empty Spaces," "Hummingbirds"
DASH Literary Journal: "On an evening with congestion in the chest"

Publisher: Leah Huete de Maines
Editor: Christen Kincaid
Cover Art: Ron Bennett
Author Photo: Photo used with permission of photographer.
Cover Design: Elizabeth Maines McCleavy

Order online: www.finishinglinepress.com
        also available on amazon.com

        Author inquiries and mail orders:
        Finishing Line Press
        PO Box 1626
        Georgetown, Kentucky 40324
        USA

Table of Contents

On an evening with congestion in the chest 1
An Ending 2
With One Eye Closed 3
Empty Nest Syndrome 4
Grasp the Wax Candle 5
Three Thrushes 6
Ode to Fishermen 7
The Poet 8
Whiskey and Anxiety 9
Heavy 10
Remember Cordoba 11
Empty Spaces 12
No One Ever 13
These eyes, they hurt me 14
Pastoral Poem 15
I did not paint 16
Questioning Pigeons 17
The Burden of Memory 18
Poem Set to Imaginary Jazz 19
Where I come from 20
A Gift 21
X 22
Hummingbirds 23
Spanish Town 24
At the feeder today 25
Ruminations 26

These poems are for you, mor

On an evening with congestion in the chest

With the full weight of the flu
sitting on my chest at 2:00 am
clogged nostrils that push a cough
through a bright red throat
I shiver the night
in a cocoon of blankets
and think
if this is what it was like

An Ending

As the marriage tears apart at the seams
they seek solace in the arms of the only comfort
either has ever known,
each other.

On a defiled marriage bed,
as an addict seeks relief
from the stranglehold of desire
in the warm comfort of heroin

and pray with the morning sun
that this life, a delirious bad dream
can be clean
as fresh linen
as once was
in the early light.

With One Eye Closed

With one eye closed
I stare at the drop of liquid
hanging not an inch above
my one eye open
meant to sooth and comfort
the bleariness of a New Year's Day
and I am anxious
and I wait for the weight of liquid
to break free
with burn and shock
a surprise
before clarity
returns
soothed
I can see
once again.

Empty Nest Syndrome

The backyard is empty this afternoon
the bird feeder is full, still
after learning from the radio
that the scientists
have estimated that 30% of all birds
have disappeared in the last forty years.

This news from afar
no doubt statistically pored over and accurate
leaves me lonely
for what I did not know
an hour before.

How am I supposed to make sense of this emptiness
as the sun sets through empty trees
a filtered, dying light
on what is no longer there,
and the yard is quiet
as if my children have gone away
far, far away.

Grasp the Wax Candle

Grasp the wax candle by the throat
careful not to burn your dainty hand
the Ivory-billed glides, smooth, free
unlike her jumpy red head sister
skin cool, feather soft
and I am where I once was
perhaps where I will always be,
in the mind's eye
of the last generation
trying my luck,
tree to naked tree.

Three Thrushes

Three tiny thrushes,
lost in the river cane
tell me
in their language,
which I've come to understand,
that none of this is my fault.

Well some of it, maybe, of course,
but certainly not all.

And yet as I look out
over the still dark lake,
silent on the matter,
I'm not sure that I believe three thrushes.

Ode to Fishermen

Fishermen from the marsh
drag solitary nets,
and pull gold from the Gulf,
brown and white and lovely
from under the May moon.
Hard, lined faces,
sculpted by poverty and salt wind,
smile, smoke, and press on
into the Gulf
under a bloated moon in May.

The Poet

What have you seen
        on your journey within?

A shaman in our time
I who art thee
can only use words
to paint what cannot be seen
in the vain desire
to apply salve
on the pulsing wound of the night
when she speaks bird languages

        that I struggle to understand
and the moon, the moon
        honey old friend
has finally decided, to love another
and so it goes

along a yellow road
in Spain

at midnight.

Whiskey and Anxiety

Whiskey and anxiety
offer little in the form of a substitute
for the ocean's swells

It's been too long
and my body whispers to the soul
all of her secrets that await nightfall
in the warm liquid of the sea

But I am deep within the land now
yet to hear a cuckoo in the wild

I have seen the roadrunner though
and even though your science tell me
that the two are one
I'll have to see the evidence
before I believe any of your fables

Heavy

I'm as heavy as I've ever been
in this, my fifty first year of life
weighed down by memories
and one too many good meals.

The bubble in the vein of the right leg
threatens to blow
with every walk in the woods
while one rash or another
linger in the closet
a distant relative
waiting to show up unannounced
at midnight.

My dreams are now populated
with refugees and exiles
far, far from here
and the birds, when they do decide to arrive
no longer allow me to fly.

Remember Cordoba

Remember the parador in Córdoba
the city alight below
but it wasn't the wine that united
nor separated us
for this was after Lisbon
where you were jealous
of the language of poets and artists
at the cafés at night
and I had to interpret their secrets
again
and the pines and sand
reminded us of the Gulf Coast
of Mississippi
far, so very far away
and we looked out and above
the blue sea
each of us
on a pilgrimage of our own making.

Empty Spaces

Deep within the empty space
of a nightingale's eye,
below the hollow where our tears gather,
I have bathed,
and cleansed my pride.

When the hyacinth and the turtle,
alone and together deep within this, the longest of nights,
gather sixteen fishes from the sea in nets of tranquility,
quickly
before the day pierces the moon with shadows,
and the nightingale dies,
alone.

No One Ever

No one ever
tells you how to feel
when your middle aged brain
cannot grasp
why you hadn't heard from your daughter
in over a month.

No one explains
how to deal with nights awake
lying next to your wife
hot with menopause and anxiety
alone.

Or what is one to do with all this time
so much time
now that there's so little left.

No one ever explained
the effort it takes
to understand the language of birds
or salve of salt air
after restless nights
in middle age.

These eyes, they hurt me

These eyes, they hurt me
deep within a head of dust
perhaps they've look out
too far this time
trying to see in vain
the lone cow across the pasture
from the electric fence.

Maybe they've refuse to look inward
into the shell of the barn
that gives the air
the shape of the barn.

Pastoral Poem

I wish to write a pastoral poem
about the city
describe the asphalt and concrete
as dirt roads, wooden fences
and of course,
haystacks and barns.

But this will never work,
I whisper to myself,
For you have already broken the first command.

I've gone and told you,
gentle reader,
what I wish to say,
and we both know,
you and I,
that whether or not
I prepare a poem
that describes buildings of steel
scraping the bottom of the sky
or two lovers in the hay behind the white farm house
under a crescent moon in Autumn
the job of interpreter
lies with you
gentle reader.

I did not paint

I did not paint
the early evening chirps
of crickets and locusts
in that last poem.

Nor how the sky is white and pink on a horizon
of pine trees across the way
mirrored on the glass lake.

Still, water gentle splash, still
rings always move out, never in.

A bird in the distance,
an owl calls a mate,
like a woman's body
curves in ways
nature struggles to replicate.

Early summer heat
remains in the air and in the loins
of memory.

Questioning Pigeons

Why would a pigeon
choose to live in the housing project
when he could simply fly the short distance
across the tracks
and live in the neighborhoods of plush and splendor

Why would a pigeon
choose to live in the ghetto
witness to pure misery
and man's lack of humanity
when on the other side of the wall
barbed wire not holding him in
he would find fields, trees, worms and friends

And the pigeon
not amused by this line of questioning
says
"Mind your own damn business,
and I'll mind mine."

The Burden of Memory

Arriving at Charles de Gaulle
as a wide eyed student
the field were alive with rabbits.
More than I had ever dared to dream
as the plane landed amongst the fields
in the early morning mist.

Later in years
I came across a letter
my father had written to his parents
as a young soldier in Europe
away from home for the first time.

He asked to pass along to his brother
"Tell Bumpsy that there are more rabbits here
than you could ever hope to imagine."

Now, very many years later
I have returned to Paris
and I find the fields of my youth, gone.
Uncle Bumpsy's been gone.
My father, gone.
And of course the rabbits are no more
and I am left to carry the burden of memory.

Poem Set to Imaginary Jazz

Black night
black and white photograph
white light, white heat
from the corner of a streetlamp
city wet, slick,
and the street a mirror
reflecting the club's neon light
wet like my skin
sweating whiskey
smelling whiskey
white light, black night
black like my skin
wet sounds pulsate
prickle
sway
thump
rom this club
tonight
black wet white.

Where I come from

I come from the delicious burn in the nose
of crawfish boiling on a Spring afternoon.

I come from predawn coffee in the kitchen of my uncle
waiting nervously for light to come,
so that we can go fishing.

The dirty sweet smell of marsh
after a summer rain.

I come from midnight on a winter's night,
lying in bed and listening to the whistle of tugs
on the river only a mile away.

The girl with the long black hair a grade above mine
who offers to share her popcorn
on the school playground.
It was then, I felt what a tingle was.

I come from a place
where we learned to drive in the railway yard.
The one with a single persimmon tree
that produced fruit that would pucker your mouth
as if forever.

I knew incense in sacred places
before I knew the smell of patchouli.
That, of course, came later.

And woods and fields
before I knew the roads
that led me here,
far away
from where I came from.

A Gift

I returned home to a gift,
jet lagged and strung out
in the immediate predawn morning.
Budapest is so very far away
but not so far behind.
I sat on the porch and watched
as a hummingbird approached
the still empty feeder
and chirped a song of welcome.
Welcome home, where is my breakfast?
Do hummingbirds chirp?
The gift of first times.
Tomorrow my friend,
you will have nectar,
sweetened by wait and desire.

X

In the grey rain this morning
I saw very many swallows
Dancing amongst flying insects

I'll try to drown depression today
But I'm afraid
That depression
Has learned to swim

Hummingbirds

A waxing moon and a pair of hummingbirds
visited our yard yesterday evening
and the clivia by the pond dripped nectar
while the season is heavy with the smell
of pasta on a low heat in the kitchen
by the open window.

I wish to get away
and walk the woods, alone
and free myself of this burden
of imagination.

Spanish Town

The smell of approaching rain
and new wet paint
aged wood
lush, overgrown yards
fecund earth
alive, bright
yellows, reds, blues
the heavy scented breeze
against the face
of an old grey dog
too tired to walk
and I forgot to forget
to not think of you.

At the feeder today

A red cockaded woodpecker
came to the feeder today
and the doves, cardinals and others
who normally frequent the free meal
did not seem to mind the outsider.

I thought it strange though
this custom of birds
like the way crows can weep around their dead kin
and simply fly away, to mourn no more
while we
are continuously tied to regret
and are thus
incapable of flight.

Ruminations

The spring birds arrive
as they always do
and death's rattle
shakes in time
once again

        Once you've changed
        a single letter in your name
        and now we are confronted
        with the person born
        whom we've never met

                Waiting and waiting
                sitting staring
                waiting
                check the time and wait
                for the wait to end

        The leaves the leaves
        glow green in the sun
        down the turning path we go
        a shadow lane is dirt
        and down we go

The Stones can do Cherry Oh Baby
and she has moved down island
accompanied by an older man
and I receive the news
as the volcano blew again today

    The knowledgeable ones have decided
    that hurricane season was too short after all
    and the average summer temperatures
    were short of average
    next they'll want to play with who I am

She flew back today
leaving only memories
that strain taught against the past
and hold together
the remains of family

    The middle ages
    don't so much divide
    a life into equal halves
    rather the era is there to remind us
    be wary of an uncertain future

Raymond Berthelot is the District Manager over State Historic Sites with the Louisiana Office of State Parks, and has worked with the Park Service for over twenty five years. Mr. Berthelot also serves as an adjunct faculty member with Baton Rouge Community College, where he teaches a course on Louisiana History.

Originally from New Orleans, Mr. Berthelot worked in the Archives Department at Xavier University of Louisiana for several years before moving to Baton Rouge. While at Xavier he was the Co-production editor of *Xavier Review Press*. At *Xavier Review Press* Mr. Berthelot oversaw the translation of the first works of Honduran poet Marco Tulio del Arca published in the United States, compiled the index to *Chester Himes: An Annotated Primary and Secondary Bibliography*, by Michel Fabre and Robert Skinner, and saw his own short stories and poems published by *La Prensa*, in Honduras. His first nonfiction, "La Fiesta Brava as Art," appeared in *The World of English* (Beijing, China), in an issue that also included an article by Nelson Mandela. Mr. Berthelot has gone on to publish several more articles, reviews, and poems, including most recently in the *Journal of Caribbean Literatures, The Carolina Quarterly* and *DASH Literary Journal*. *The Middle Ages* is Mr. Berthelot's first chapbook of collected poetry.

Raymond Berthelot holds an M.A. in History from Louisiana State University and two B.A.s, Political Science and History, from the University of New Orleans. Mr. Berthelot is married to Gerardina Berthelot, of La Ceiba, Honduras, and together they have one daughter, Oriana. When not travelling, Mr. and Mrs. Berthelot make their home in Baton Rouge, Louisiana, along with Luna and Lily Rose.

www.ingramcontent.com/pod-product-compliance
Lightning Source LLC
LaVergne TN
LVHW041514070426
835507LV00012B/1553